94140010R00061

Made in the USA
Lexington, KY
24 July 2018